Cambridge **Discovery Education**™
▶ **INTERACTIVE READERS**

Series editor: Bob Hastings

THREE IN ONE
THE CHALLENGE
OF THE TRIATHLON

A2

Genevieve Kocienda

CAMBRIDGE
UNIVERSITY PRESS

DISCOVERY
EDUCATION™

CAMBRIDGE UNIVERSITY PRESS
Cambridge, New York, Melbourne, Madrid, Cape Town,
Singapore, São Paulo, Delhi, Mexico City

Cambridge University Press
32 Avenue of the Americas, New York, NY 10013-2473, USA

www.cambridge.org
Information on this title: www.cambridge.org/9781107622555

First published 2014

Printed in Hong Kong, China, by Golden Cup Printing Company Limited

A catalog record for this publication is available from the British Library.

Library of Congress Cataloging-in-Publication Data

Kocienda, G.
  Three in one : the challenge of the triathlon / Genevieve Kocienda.
     pages cm. -- (Cambridge discovery interactive readers)
  ISBN 978-1-107-62255-5 (pbk. : alk. paper)
  1. Triathlon--Juvenile literature. 2. English language--Textbooks for foreign speakers.
  3. Readers (Elementary) I. Title.

GV1060.73.K64 2014
796.42'57--dc23

2013016507

ISBN 978-1-107-62255-5

Additional resources for this publication at www.cambridge.org

Layout services, art direction, book design, and photo research: Q2ABillSMITH GROUP
Editorial services: Hyphen S.A.
Audio production: CityVox, New York
Video production: Q2ABillSMITH GROUP

Contents

Before You Read:
Get Ready!

Do you like to swim, ride a bike, and run? How about doing all three, one after the other?

Words to Know

Complete the sentences with the correct words.

cycle	equipment	competition	strength	athlete

1 You need _____ to carry something heavy.

2 Most people can _____ faster than they can walk.

3 An _____ must be strong and healthy.

4 A running race is a kind of _____.

5 To run in a race, you need special _____ such as running shoes.

Words to Know

Read the paragraph. Then complete the sentences with the correct highlighted words.

A marathon is a running race that is 42 kilometers long. You need strength and endurance to compete in sporting events like marathons. But there are also extreme races which are longer than marathons. They take place in many countries around the world. Some races are 84 kilometers long! To run that far you need to train a lot.

1 If you can do something for a long time, you have

_____ .

2 An _____ race is a very long or difficult race.

3 In a race, athletes _____ against each other to be the fastest.

4 The race will _____ at 8:00 tomorrow morning.

5 There are lots of sporting _____ here every summer.

6 Athletes often _____ many days a week for big races.

CHAPTER 1

Three Sports in One Event

THE WORD TRIATHLON IS FROM GREEK. *TRI* MEANS "THREE" AND *ATHLOS* IS SOMETHING BIG AND IMPORTANT THAT YOU HAVE ACHIEVED.

A triathlon is a very difficult sports **competition**. A triathlon is three **events** in one: swimming, cycling, and running. The athletes, called triathletes, compete against each other in each part, or leg, of the competition and in two transition[1] times. The first transition time is when the triathletes go from the water to the bike. The second transition time is from cycling to running.

How long is a triathlon? Well, in an Olympic triathlon, competitors swim 1500 meters, cycle 43 kilometers, and run 10 kilometers. That may sound hard, but the famous Ironman triathlons are longer: a 3.8-kilometer swim, 180 kilometers on the bike, and then a full 42-kilometer marathon!

The longest triathlon in the world is called the Ultraman World Championship. It is a three-day, 515-kilometer race held on the Big Island of Hawaii.

[1]**transition:** a change from one thing to another thing

The transition from swimming to cycling

The Ultraman

Day 1: swim for 10 kilometers and cycle
for 145 kilometers

Day 2: cycle for 276 kilometers

Day 3: a double marathon – 84 kilometers!

It takes a lot of strength and **endurance** to do the Ultraman. Only 35 triathletes are invited to compete each year.

The Xterra is a famous off-road triathlon. In off-road triathlons, the cycling and running legs are more difficult than usual. Competitors go through trees, over rocks, logs,[2] and rivers, and up and down mountains. They are never on a road. The competitors need special bikes, and they can't go fast because the course[3] is so difficult.

[2]**log:** a large piece of wood from a tree
[3]**course:** the path that all competitors follow in a race

Triathlons take place all over the world: deserts,[4] mountains, small towns, big cities. One of the most difficult triathlons is the Norseman Xtreme Triathlon in Hardangerfjord, Norway.

The triathletes in this competition swim 3.8 kilometers in water that is 15.5° Celsius.[5] After that, they cycle 180 kilometers and then run 42.2 kilometers up a mountain. The last 17.2 kilometers of the mountain run is an **extreme** climb up to 1,850 meters! The race is so difficult and so dangerous that the competitors cannot go on the mountain alone. They must have helpers follow them in a car with food, water, and clothes.

In 2012, Henrik Oftedal of Norway won this competition with the best time in the race's history: 10 hours, 23 minutes, and 24 seconds.

[4]**desert:** a very hot and dry place with very few plants, like the Sahara in Africa

[5]**15.5° Celsius:** fifteen point five degrees Celsius

Triathletes compete in age groups. Each man or woman competes against the other athletes in his or her group.

Because the competitors are amateurs,[6] they are not in it for money. They practice and compete for many different reasons: to get stronger, to test their endurance, to be healthy, or just to have fun.

Some triathletes compete for special reasons. When Jenn Sommermann was 41, her doctor told her she was very sick. Jenn was lucky: she didn't die. But she wanted to get money to help other people who were sick like her. She decided to compete in 50 triathlons in all 50 states in the United States in 2013. She wants to raise $100,000.

Jenn Sommermann competes for personal reasons.

....

[6]**amateur:** doing something as a hobby, not as a job

? **EVALUATE**
Triathlons are very difficult. Why do you think people do them?

CHAPTER 2

The Ironman

THE IRONMAN IS THE WORLD'S
MOST FAMOUS TRIATHLON.

The first Ironman race took place in 1978 in Honolulu, Hawaii. There were 12 competitors, and the winner finished in 11 hours, 46 minutes, and 58 seconds. Today, there are 28 Ironman Triathlons in different places around the world, but the World Ironman Championships are held in Kona, Hawaii.

Who first had the idea for an Ironman triathlon?

There was already a long bike race, a long swim race, and a marathon in Hawaii, but not all three events together on the same day. In 1977, US Navy Commander John Collins decided to test the strength and endurance of the athletes from these races. He said that a person who can win all three races – a 3.8-kilometer swim, a 180-kilometer bike ride, and a 42-kilometer run – is an "Iron Man."

In 1982, the Ironman competition became famous. Julie Moss was in first place in the women's race.

ANALYZE

Why did Julie Moss's finish make the Ironman triathlon famous?

A few meters before the end of the race, she fell down, exhausted.[7] Kathleen McCartney won the race, but Moss crawled over the finish line on her hands and knees.

There are many other inspiring[8] stories about Ironman competitors. One example is father and son, Dick and Rick Hoyt. Rick has a medical problem, and he can't use his legs or arms. His father pulls Rick in a special boat for the swimming leg. For the biking leg, he carries Rick in a special seat in front of the bicycle. Finally, Dick runs and pushes Rick in a wheelchair in the last leg. They have completed six Ironman Triathlons together.

Dick and Rick Hoyt

[7]**exhausted:** dangerously tired

[8]**inspiring:** making someone want to learn or do something

CHAPTER 3

Swimming

SWIMMING IS THE FIRST, AND MOST DIFFICULT, LEG OF A TRIATHLON.

Many triathletes think that the swimming leg of a triathlon is the hardest. But why? One reason is that most triathletes are runners or cyclists first, not swimmers.

Swimming is the most technical[9] leg of the race. Most athletes know the correct way to ride a bike or run in a competition, but swimming correctly and fast is a new skill[10] for them to learn. They have to **train** harder to swim well than to run or cycle well.

Also, the swimming leg usually takes place outside in "open water," such as a large lake or even the ocean.

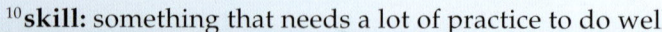

[9]**technical:** needing a special way of doing something
[10]**skill:** something that needs a lot of practice to do well

When they train, most athletes run and cycle outside, the same as in a triathlon. However, they usually train for the swimming leg in a swimming pool, indoors. Sometimes, the weather makes it impossible to train in open water.

New triathletes soon learn that swimming in a pool is very different from swimming in open water. In a swimming pool, there are often only a few other people around them. They have enough space to move easily. The water is warm and there are no currents,[11] so it is easy to swim in a straight line.

Swimming in open water is much harder. There are waves and currents. The water can be very cold. And in a triathlon, you are not alone. There are many people swimming all together. There are arms and legs everywhere!

[11] **current:** a movement of water or air

Triathletes running through waves into the sea

Another difficulty with swimming is navigation.[12] When you run or cycle, it's easy to stay in a straight line. You can see the side of the road and any changes in the road in front of you. When you swim in open water, you cannot see the way very well. While you're swimming, you must look for special signs that show the way, and that's not easy.

In some triathlons, the competitors never get to practice in the open water. For example, in the New York City Ironman Triathlon, the 3.8-kilometer swim takes place in the Hudson River. It is the only day of the year that anyone can swim in the river. So, competitors have no idea how it feels to swim in the Hudson until the day of the competition.

[12]**navigation:** finding your way

The swimming leg can also be the most dangerous leg of the race. 23 people died in triathlons from 2004 to 2008, and 18 of these people died during the swimming leg.

This is easy to understand when you think about it. If a competitor faints[13] or has a heart problem during the running or cycling legs, people see that there is a problem and can help the person immediately. In the water, however, if a competitor faints, the person goes under the water. It is more difficult to help the person. Before help arrives, the person can easily drown.[14]

[13] **faint:** not feel well and fall down
[14] **drown:** die in the water because you cannot take air into your body

Video Quest

Training for a Triathlon, Part 1

Watch the video to hear Rian Gonzalez talk about training for a triathlon. Why does he want to compete?

CHAPTER 4

Biking

MANY TRIATHLETES WERE CYCLISTS BEFORE THEY BECAME TRIATHLETES, BUT THE BIKE LEG OF A TRIATHLON CAN STILL BE DIFFICULT FOR THEM.

The bike leg is the second leg of a triathlon. It has the farthest **distance** and usually takes about 50 percent of the race time. Most triathletes train hardest for this leg.

Triathletes also need the right equipment for cycling: a good bicycle, of course, but also special cycling shoes, a bike helmet for their heads, and special bottles for their water and sports drinks.

Triathletes practice putting on their bike equipment. Remember, the clock does not stop between legs of the competition. Part of the triathlon is how fast competitors make the transition from one leg to another. They must change from their swimsuits to their bike equipment very quickly.

The bike leg in a triathlon is often very hard; for example, the 89.6-kilometer bike leg in the SavageMan Triathlon in Maryland, USA. The greatest test of strength and endurance in this race is the famous "Westernport Wall." After cycling 29.7 kilometers, competitors have to climb this hill, the steepest hill in any triathlon. It has a 31 percent grade!

Westernport Wall is a very steep hill.

The Westernport Wall is so steep that most competitors – even professional triathletes – must get off their bikes and walk! It is so hard that any competitor who can stay on the bike all the way gets a special prize. The competitor's name is written on a brick and put in the road.

A brick

Video Quest

Training for a Triathlon, Part 2

Watch this video to see how Rian trains for the bike leg. What does Rian learn from his **coach**?

CHAPTER 5

Running

RUNNING IS THE LAST LEG OF A TRIATHLON. COMPETITORS GET OFF THEIR BIKES AND CHANGE INTO RUNNING SHOES AS FAST AS THEY CAN.

Many runners like to do triathlons. So, the running leg is probably easy for them, right? Wrong! Running comes after the competitors swim and then cycle a long, long way. Their legs are already very tired. The change from biking to running can feel extreme.

New triathletes are very surprised by how weak[15] and heavy their legs feel when it is time to run. They are surprised by how slowly they run. It feels like they have someone else's legs! Triathletes often practice this transition so they can start running the last leg sooner.

[15]**weak:** not strong

The running leg of the Arch to Arc triathlon

Running on sand is very difficult.

In some triathlons the run is even more difficult. In the Superfrog half-triathlon, part of the running course is on a beach. Amazingly, some triathletes enjoy running on the soft sand!

The extreme Enduroman Arch to Arc triathlon, which goes from London, England, to Paris, France, is a little different. Competitors run first, then swim, then cycle. But that doesn't make the event any easier. The running leg is really long – 140 kilometers from London to Dover.

Do you think 140 kilometers is the hardest running **challenge**? Well, it's not. For triathletes who want more, there is the Deca Enduroman Challenge. That's like an ironman triathlon every day for ten days in a row.[16] Over ten days the competitors have to run 421 kilometers!

[16] **in a row:** one after another without a break

Video Quest

The Big Event

Watch this video about Rian's triathlon. Rian didn't win the triathlon. Why does he feel great?

CHAPTER 6

What Do You Think?

WOULD YOU LIKE TO COMPETE IN A TRIATHLON?

Abu Dhabi, UAE

Wales, UK

Are you a competitive person? Do you enjoy competing against people you know, like friends or family members? Does competing with others make work or schoolwork more interesting to you? Why or why not?

Read about these three triathlons. Then think about these questions:

- Which one would you like to do?

- Why would you do it?

- How much do you think you have to train for it?

The Chicago Triathlon, USA

This is a sprint, or short, triathlon. There is a 0.75-kilometer swim, a 22-kilometer bike ride, and a 5-kilometer run. It is a very popular race and takes competitors on a tour of the great city of Chicago, USA.

ANALYZE

Think about the people who compete in triathlons. How are they the same? How might they be different from each other?

Chicago, Illinois, USA

The Abu Dhabi International Triathlon, UAE

Do you think you can finish a triathlon alone? No? You and two friends can do the Abu Dhabi triathlon together. One person swims 1500 meters, one person cycles 100 kilometers, and one person runs 10 kilometers. You can enjoy the beautiful city of Abu Dhabi during the race and then, if you're not tired and you want more, you can take a tour of the desert after the race.

The Brutal Double Ultra Triathlon, Wales, UK

This extreme triathlon takes place in the beautiful Welsh countryside. You swim 7.7 kilometers in cold Lake Padarn, cycle 360 kilometers on a very hilly road, and then run 84 kilometers up and down the tallest mountain in Wales.

So, which triathlon is for you?

After You Read

Read the sentences and choose Ⓐ True or Ⓑ False.

1 Cycling is usually the first leg of a triathlon.
- Ⓐ True
- Ⓑ False

2 The Ultraman Triathlon takes three days.
- Ⓐ True
- Ⓑ False

3 Triathlons are always the same distance.
- Ⓐ True
- Ⓑ False

4 For most people, swimming is the most difficult leg in a triathlon.
- Ⓐ True
- Ⓑ False

5 Rian Gonzalez is afraid of putting his face in the water.
- Ⓐ True
- Ⓑ False

6 The transitions from leg to leg are not important in a triathlon.
- Ⓐ True
- Ⓑ False

7 Triathletes need special biking shoes.
- Ⓐ True
- Ⓑ False

8 The running leg is difficult because most triathletes are swimmers, not runners.
- Ⓐ True
- Ⓑ False

Match

Match the vocabulary with the correct definitions.

Words	Definitions
① cycle ___ ② equipment ___ ③ competition ___ ④ strength ___ ⑤ athlete ___ ⑥ compete ___ ⑦ extreme ___ ⑧ endurance ___ ⑨ distance ___	a. if you have this you are strong b. how close or far something is c. someone who is good at sports d. to ride a bicycle e. to try to win a race f. what you have when you are able to do something for a long time g. an event where people try to win something h. very great; the most or worst i. the things you use in a triathlon

Answer the Questions

Read pages 6–15 again and answer the questions.

❶ What is the longest triathlon in the world?

_____

_____

❷ What is an off-road triathlon?

_____

_____

❸ Why did Jenn Sommermann want to compete in marathons?

_____

_____

❹ Why is the swimming leg the most dangerous?

_____

_____

23

Answer Key

Words to Know, page 4
1 strength **2** cycle **3** athlete **4** competition
5 equipment

Words to Know, page 5
1 endurance **2** extreme **3** compete **4** take place
5 events **6** train

Evaluate, page 9 *Answers will vary.*

Analyze, page 11 *Answers will vary.*

Video Quest, page 15 He wants to be healthier.

Video Quest, page 17
He learns how to fit a bike to his body. He learns the right
way to ride a bike.

Video Quest, page 19
He was afraid he wouldn't finish, but he did.

Analyze, page 21 *Answers will vary.*

True or False, page 22
1 B **2** A **3** B **4** A **5** A **6** B **7** A **8** B

Match, page 23
1 d **2** i **3** g **4** a **5** c **6** e **7** h **8** f **9** b

Answer the Questions, page 23
1 the Ultraman World Championship

2 The bike and run legs are not on a course or roads;
they are through woods or other natural places.

3 to raise money to help other people who are sick.

4 If a person faints in the water, they can drown easily.